The Complete Keto Diet for Beginners 2019-2020

Easy Keto Recipes to Reset Your Body and Live a Healthy Life (How You Lose 38 Pounds in 30-Day)

Dr Peter Henery

Table of contents

Introduction

Here's in this book we have to learn all about the ketogenic diet from basics. We have seen how the ketogenic diet is different from other diet and what are the health benefits of the diet in detail with enjoying different types of delicious and healthy keto recipes.

Keto diet is also known as a low carb diet which is high in fats and adequate amount of protein consumption. Keto diet is not just diet plan it's a healthy eating habit for your body. Normally our body uses glucose as a primary source of energy. Compare to another diet ketogenic diet is easier to follow. While you are on a ketogenic diet your body breaks down fats for energy instead of glucose. The ketogenic diet is metabolically flexible because it easily switches between glucose to fat burning. Compare to other diet keto diet is more restrictive regarding carb intake. Carb intake will increase your blood sugar level. Keto diet is carb restrictive diet so it maintains your blood sugar level. Keto diet is very effective on type-2 diabetes and it also treats various conditions like epilepsy, Alzheimer's, Parkinson's, high blood pressure, metabolic syndrome, etc. keto diet is not just improving your physical health but it is also improving your mental health.

My goal here is that you should understand the ketogenic diet, its various health benefits, and science behind the ketogenic diet. After reading this book I hope you will understand how the ketogenic diet works and during the ketogenic diet which food to eat and which food to avoid. There are also tips given for successful keto diet. I hope the information found in this book definitely enrich your life.

Chapter1: The Basics of The Keto Diet

What is the Keto Diet?

To perform daily operations our body needs energy and these energies come in the form of carbohydrates, proteins, and fats. The keto diet is low in carbohydrates, high in fats and need an adequate amount of proteins. It's not just a diet plan but it also changes you're eating habit to consume natural and healthy food and makes you stronger physically and mentally. Normally our body uses glucose as a primary source of energy. Keto diet is basically low carbohydrate diet lowering carb intake helps to push your body into the state of ketosis.

Ketosis is the state of the body in which our body breaks down fats in the liver for fuel instead of glucose. Keto diet very effective on rapid weight loss and also helps to the treatment of epilepsy.

How keto is different from other diets

- Regarding carbohydrate intake, the keto diet is more restrictive than any other diet.
- Keto diet is very effective for rapid weight loss to compare to any other diet. Keto diet helps to burn body fats very effectively when your body is in a ketosis state.
- Keto diet is very effective on various diseases it provides long term health benefits. It is very effective on epilepsy, Parkinson's disease, metabolic syndrome, high blood pressure, and type-2 diabetes. It also helps to treat mental disorders.
- In ketogenic diet 75 percent of calories are consumed from body fats, 20 percent of calories come from proteins and 5 percent of calories come from carbs.

How does the ketogenic diet work?

The main purpose of the diet is to decrease carbohydrates intake and increase fat intake. Normally our body uses glucose as a primary energy source. When you are on a keto diet your body breaks down fats for energy instead of glucose. This glucose is stored into the body muscles and tissues in the form of glycogens. When glycogen level is increased in our body then excess glycogens are converted into fats and stored in our liver.

When you are reducing carb intake this will affect to reduce glycogen storage and hormonal insulin level also decreases. During this process, fatty acids are released from stored body fats and the liver converts it into ketones. Ketones are one kind of acid travel through your bloodstream and your body muscles and tissues use it as a fuel. When carb intake is reduced your body goes into a metabolic state called ketosis. In this condition, your body breaks down fats for energy instead of carbohydrates (glucose).

How to know when you are in Ketosis

There are various symptoms you have seen when your body enters into the state of ketosis these symptoms are described as follows.

- Bad Breath Problem: This problem basically occurs due to acetone. Bad breath is one of the common side effects occurs during the fat breaking process. It releases acetone through your mouth and due to this bad breath problem occurs. Normally this problem is occurring during the first some week. This ensures that you are in the state of ketosis.

- Increase Thirst and Dry Mouth: Dry mouth and increase thirst is one of the common side effects occurs during a ketogenic diet. During ketosis, urination is increased due to this reason it increases your thirst. Another reason is when insulin level in your body decreases due to this your kidney release water and sodium from your body. Dry mouth and increase in thirst are one of the signs which indicate that you are in ketosis.

- Quick and Rapid Weight Loss: Rapid weight loss is happening because your body shedding excess water and stored carbohydrates due to this reason your weight decreases rapidly. This will happen during the first week of the ketogenic diet and rapid weight loss is also one of the symptoms which indicate that you are in ketosis.

- Increased Urination: During the first week of diet you will notice that increase in urination. This will happen because of losing glycogens from your body. While you are on ketogenic diet glucose level is decreased in your body. Glycogen contains 3 to 4 part of the water in it and due to this reason, your urination increases during a ketogenic diet. This is one of the reasons indicates you are in ketosis.

- Insomnia: This is one of the common symptoms during a ketogenic diet. Many peoples who follow a ketogenic diet face insomnia and waking at night during first time change in diet. This condition improves after some weeks.

The Health Benefits of Keto diet

Keto diet has various health benefits which are described as follows:

- Effective Weight Loss: This is one of the major benefits of a ketogenic diet. Normally our body uses glucose as a primary energy source. This glucose is stored in the form of glycogens. Then excess glycogens are converted into the fats. Keto diet is carb restrictive diet due to this carb intake is low and the glucose level is also decreased. In this case, your body breaks down fats for energy due to this your body weight reduces rapidly and the keto diet is very effective for long term weight loss benefits.

- Improves your brain functions: Keto diet is very effective in improving your brain health and your brain functions. Most of the research and study shows that a keto diet is helpful to reduce the risk of Alzheimer's, epilepsy, Parkinson's and neurodegeneration disease. When the level of insulin and glucose is decreased your liver produces ketones from fatty acids. These ketones provide near about 70 percent of energy to your brain to perform day to day operations.

- Maintain your blood sugar level: During a ketogenic diet, your body uses ketones as a primary energy source instead of glucose. To transport into cell glucose needs insulin it also increases insulin sensitivity. On the other side, ketones don't require insulin to transport. It indicates that the keto diet prevents insulin resistance. This will help to maintain your blood sugar level stable throughout the day.

- Boost your athletic performance: Keto diet does not only reduce the weight but also it helps to improve your athletic performance. According to scientific research study, it proves that the keto diet helps to reduce your weight, it also helps to maintain your muscle mass and reduce body fats. It also helps to improve your body composition.

- **Helps to Treat/Prevent various disease:** In keto, diet ketones are used as a primary energy source. These ketones have anti-inflammatory and antioxidants properties. It will help to prevent/treat various diseases like Parkinson's, Alzheimer's, type-2 diabetes, heart-related disease, and cancer. The research and study show that keto diet starves cancer cell in your body this is happening due to the reduction of carbohydrates from your diet. Cancer cells cannot metabolically shift to use fat for energy instead of glucose.

- **Improves metabolic flexibility:** Normally our body cells use glucose as a primary energy source. While you are on a keto diet your body burn fats instead of glucose for energy. Ketones are used as a fuel for your body and brain. This change happens in your body cells can be metabolically flexible. Metabolic flexibility helps your body to switch in between carb and fats for fuel.

- **Anti-aging properties:** when you are in the state of ketosis your body uses ketones as a primary fuel for energy. During a keto diet, your insulin level decreases. It also helps to reduce the oxidative stress this will helps to increase your lifespan. Keto diet is carb restrictive diet low calorie can slow down the aging process.

8 Helpful Tips for the keto Journey

1. **Limit your carb consumption:** Keto diet is carb restrictive diet. You should consume below 25 grams of carb daily. Eating low carb daily will help your body to enter into a state of ketosis. Ketosis is the state of the body in which your body breaks down fats for energy instead of carbohydrates.

2. **Consume healthy fats:** While you are on a ketogenic diet you should consume plenty of healthy fats. Consuming healthy fats during a diet helps to boost ketones level in your body and push your body into the state of ketosis. Avoid bad fats like canola oil, sunflower oil, vegetable oil, etc. Use good and healthy fats like Avocado oil, coconut oil, olive oil, etc.

3. Stay hydrated: During a ketogenic diet, your body losing glycogens through urination. These glycogens hold 4 to 5 parts of water due to this your body dehydrated. You should drink plenty of water during a keto diet. This will help to stay hydrated your body. You can also consume tea, coffee and smoothie to stay your body hydrated.

4. Get enough sleep: When you are following keto diet, you should need enough sleep. Not just enough sleep you need better quality sleep for that you should sleep in a cool and dark room environment. Maintain room temperature around 65 F and sleep at least 7 hours daily at night. Inadequate sleep may increase your carving and it also affects your weight loss process.

5. Do regular exercise: When you are doing any hard work activity your ketones levels are increased. Regular exercise helps to reduce your weight and also helps to maintain your blood sugar level. Regular exercise helps you to stay energized throughout the day.

6. Consume adequate protein: While you are on a keto diet your body breaks down fats for energy. In this process your body losses muscles and fats. To maintain your muscle mass, you should consume an adequate amount of protein. You should consume 0.75 grams of protein per pound as per your body weight.

7. Use coconut oil in your diet: Coconut oil contains healthy fats called Medium Chain Triglycerides (MCTs). These MCTs are quickly absorbed directly to your liver and convert it into ketones. Coconut oil contains four types of MCTs and near about 50 percent of fats are coming from lauric acid. One of the scientific research studies proves that lauric acid helps to maintain the level of ketosis.

8. Keep your stress down: If you are suffering from chronic stress then it will difficult to stay your body into ketosis. If you take stress, then it raises your stress hormones and increases your blood sugar. You have to plan some strategies which will help you to reduce your stress and creates relaxation and peace into your life.

Chapter2: Food to Eat

In this chapter, you have seen the recommended food list for the ketogenic diet.

- Meats:

  Keto diet recommends unprocessed meats because unprocessed meats are low in carbohydrates. Grass-fed and organic meat is the best choice for a ketogenic diet. Grass-fed meat contains a huge amount of Omega-3 fatty acids. Omega-3 fatty acids are helpful to improve your heart health, reduce depression and lower level of inflammation. Dark meat is also a good choice for the keto diet because it is high in fats. Avoid processed meats because it contains added carbohydrates.

  Recommended: Pork chops, ground beef, steak, pork loin, ground pork, goat, lamb, steak, stew meats, roasts, etc.

- Seafood and Fish:

  Seafood and fish are the best sources of omega-3 fatty acids, selenium and high quality of proteins. Wild caught fish and fatty fish are one of the best choices for a ketogenic diet. Fish like salmon are rich in vitamin B, selenium and potassium.

  Recommended: Salmon, tuna, catfish, cod, mackerel, flounder, tod, crab, oyster, squid, clams, lobster, scallop, mussels, etc.

- Eggs:

  Eggs are recommended during keto diet because it is low in carbohydrates and enriched with protein. It provides an adequate amount of protein to your body.

  Recommended: Keto recommends Organic and pasteurizes eggs during the diet.

- Fruits and Vegetables:

  Most of the vegetables are low in carbohydrates and used to add flavor and texture to your keto meal. It is enriched with various essential vitamins and nutrients. Avoid starchy vegetables like yams, carrot, potatoes, and beet because they are high in carb. Non-starchy vegetables are low in carb but it is high in essential nutrients and minerals. Vegetables contain antioxidant which helps to protect against free radical.

Recommended: Fruits: Raspberries, avocado, blackberries, olives, lemon, and coconut.

Vegetables: Celery, spinach, chives, broccoli, lettuce, cucumber, kale, green beans, tomatoes, eggplant, Brussels sprout, cauliflower, bell peppers, zucchini, asparagus, cabbage, garlic, artichokes, and onion.

- Fats and oils:

Fat plays a very important role during the ketogenic diet because near about 70 to 80 percent of energy is coming from fats. Keto recommended consuming healthy fats because it contains Omega-3 fatty acids which are not produced by your body. Healthy oils contain olive oil and coconut oils they help to lower your blood pressure and also beneficial for treating Alzheimer's.

Recommended: Coconut oil, avocado oil, olive oil, lard, palm kernel oil, beef fat, butter, macadamia nut oil, sesame oil, and walnut oil.

- Dairy:

Dairy products are high in fats and also provide calcium and proteins. Keto recommends high-fat dairy products and heavy cream for cooking. Avoid low-fat dairy products which are high in carb values.

Recommended: Butter, Wiping cream, Greek yogurt, cheddar cheese, cottage cheese.

- Beverages:

Keto recommends some beverages which will help to stay you hydrated during the diet. Unsweetened Coffee and teas are carb free drinks which will help to increase your metabolism and also improves your physical and mental performance.

Recommended: Tea, coffee, coconut water, plain water, etc.

- Condiments:

Keto recommends those condiments which contain less than 5 grams of carb in each serving. You can use these condiments for cooking or dipping.

Recommended: Soy sauce, mayonnaise, lemon juice, vinegar, and hot sauce.

Chapter3: Foods to Avoid

In this chapter, we have seen the keto restricted food list.

- Added Sugar: Sugary foods contain carbs and it causes to increase your blood sugar level. Consumption of sugar also causes an insulin spike and due to this, you are kicked out from the process of ketosis. You should completely avoid fruit juice, sports drinks, vitamin water, and soft drinks. Avoid chocolate bar, cakes, breakfast cereals, candy, donuts. There are hidden sugars are present in beverages, condiments like sauces, drinks, dressings, and packed food. Also avoid Honey, maple syrup, Agave nectar, dates.

- Avoid Starchy Foods: Starchy foods are high in carb keto diet suggest to avoid these foods because it raises your blood sugar level. Keto avoids starchy food like potatoes, rice, French fries, porridge, potato chips, bread, and pasta.

- Avoid Grains: Avoid grains during keto diet will help you to reach ketosis. Here are some grains like wheat, corn, barley, buckwheat, sprouted grains, oats, rye, etc. you should not only avoid grains but also avoid products made up from grains like pasta, pizza, cookies, bread, crackers, etc.

- Avoid Tropical Fruits: Tropical fruits are high in carbs and sugar. Avoid tropical fruits like Mango, pineapple, banana, tangerine, grapes, and papaya.

- Avoid Refined oils: Refined oils contain omega-6 which can raise your blood pressure you should avoid refined oils like sunflower, canola, soybean, safflower oil. Also, avoid trans-fat like margarine during a keto diet.

- Avoid Processed Foods: Processed foods are avoided from your keto diet plan because it contains preservatives, unhealthy ingredients, and artificial colorings. Instead of eating processed food you should focus to eat fresh and nutritious food.

Chapter4: FAQs

- What is a keto diet?

  Keto diet helps to get your body into the state of ketosis. This means that your body breaks down fats for energy instead of glucose. This means that your body doesn't depend on glucose to regulate your body energy level.

- How to find I am in ketosis?

  When your body enters into ketosis it shows some sign and symptoms like bad breath, dry mouth, and increase in thirst, rapid weight loss, and frequent urination indicates that you are in ketosis.

- Is the keto diet being effective for rapid weight loss?

  Yes, when your body is in the state of ketosis it breaks down fats for energy instead of glucose. Breaking down fats will help to reduce your weight rapidly.

- How should I track my ketone level?

  There are two methods to track your ketones level.

  Ketostix: This is the easiest and inexpensive way to know your ketone levels using urine ketone strips.

  Blood Test: This is an accurate method to measure your blood ketone level. It's the same as a glucometer test but little bit costly method.

- Can I drink Alcohol on diet?

  A small amount of alcohol is ok during a keto diet. If you consume more it will affect your diet. When you are intake alcohol your body processing alcohol during this period fat burning process is stop by your body. If you want to consume alcohol during keto diet choose whiskey, vodka or wine which are very low in carbohydrates.

- What can I eat on a keto food plan?

  This is totally depending on your food allergies and sensitivity. Keto food plans are nutritionally balanced and mainly include meats, seafood's, fish, eggs, nuts and oil, low carb fruits and vegetables.

Chapter5: 30-Day Meal plan

Day 1

- Breakfast-Perfect Zucchini Muffins
- Lunch-Tasty Chicken Soup
- Dinner-Salsa Beef

Day 2

- Breakfast-Easy Breakfast Omelet Waffle
- Lunch-Garlic Asparagus Soup
- Dinner-Parmesan Pork Chops

Day 3

- Breakfast-Quick & Easy Pancakes
- Lunch-Tomato Soup
- Dinner-Greek Pork Chops

Day 4

- Breakfast-Healthy Vegetable Muffins
- Lunch-Shrimp Salad
- Dinner-Meatloaf

Day 5

- Breakfast-Spicy Egg Scrambled
- Lunch-Sautéed Shrimp with Cheese
- Dinner-Beef Stir Fry

Day 6

- Breakfast-Crust-less Breakfast Quiche
- Lunch-Easy Shrimp Skewers
- Dinner-Lamb Kebabs

Day 7

- Breakfast-Scrambled Egg Muffins
- Lunch-Spinach Soup
- Dinner-Lamb Meatloaf

Day 8

- Breakfast-Savory Breakfast Casserole
- Lunch-Broccoli Cheese Soup
- Dinner-Pork Roast

Day 9

- Breakfast-Olive Cheese Omelet
- Lunch-Celery Soup
- Dinner-Garlic Olive Pork Chops

Day 10

- Breakfast-Cheese Soufflés
- Lunch-Spicy Salmon
- Dinner-Roasted Beef

Day 11

- Breakfast-Simple Egg Loaf
- Lunch-Shrimp Cilantro Salad
- Dinner-Coconut Pork Curry

Day 12

- Breakfast-Tomato Cheese Omelet
- Lunch-Tuna Salad
- Dinner-Asian Beef Stew

Day 13

- Breakfast-Banana Breakfast Bread
- Lunch-Tasty Seasoned Shrimp
- Dinner-Baked Chicken

Day 14

- Breakfast-Cheese Bacon Muffins
- Lunch-Baked Chicken
- Dinner-Herb Marinated Chicken

Day 15

- Breakfast-Mexican Breakfast Frittata
- Lunch-Herb Marinated Chicken
- Dinner-Chicken Thighs

Day 16

- Breakfast-Perfect Zucchini Muffins
- Lunch-Chicken Thighs
- Dinner-Balsamic Chicken

Day 17

- Breakfast-Easy Breakfast Omelet Waffle
- Lunch-Lemon Butter Scallops
- Dinner-Grilled Chicken

Day 18

- Breakfast-Quick & Easy Pancakes
- Lunch-Delicious Fish Stew
- Dinner-Lemon Butter Chicken Piccata

Day 19

- Breakfast-Healthy Vegetable Muffins
- Lunch-Shrimp Dinner

- Dinner-Paprika Chicken

Day 20

- Breakfast-Spicy Egg Scrambled
- Lunch-Balsamic Chicken
- Dinner-Salsa Beef

Day 21

- Breakfast-Crust-less Breakfast Quiche
- Lunch-Paprika Chicken
- Dinner-Parmesan Pork Chops

Day 22

- Breakfast-Scrambled Egg Muffins
- Lunch-Creamy Chicken Basil Salad
- Dinner-Greek Pork Chops

Day 23

- Breakfast-Savory Breakfast Casserole
- Lunch-Tasty Chicken Soup
- Dinner-Meatloaf

Day 24

- Breakfast-Olive Cheese Omelet
- Lunch-Spinach Soup
- Dinner-Beef Stir Fry

Day 25

- Breakfast-Cheese Soufflés
- Lunch-Broccoli Cheese Soup
- Dinner-Lamb Kebabs

Day 26

- Breakfast-Simple Egg Loaf
- Lunch-Celery Soup
- Dinner-Lamb Meatloaf

Day 27

- Breakfast-Tomato Cheese Omelet
- Lunch-Grilled Chicken
- Dinner-Pork Roast

Day 28

- Breakfast-Banana Breakfast Bread
- Lunch-Lemon Butter Chicken Piccata
- Dinner-Garlic Olive Pork Chops

Day 29

- Breakfast-Cheese Bacon Muffins
- Lunch-Chicken Avocado Salad
- Dinner-Roasted Beef

Day 30

- Breakfast-Mexican Breakfast Frittata
- Lunch-Chicken Curried Salad
- Dinner-Coconut Pork Curry

Chapter6: Breakfast

Perfect Zucchini Muffins

Preparation Time: 10 minutes
Cooking Time: 35 minutes
Serve: 12

Ingredients:

- 4 eggs
- 1 tsp baking powder
- 1 cup almond flour
- 1/3 cup sour cream
- 5 oz ham, diced
- ¾ cup parmesan cheese, grated
- 1 zucchini, grated
- ¼ tsp pepper
- ½ tsp salt

Directions:

1. Preheat the oven to 350 F/ 180 C.
2. Spray a muffin tray with cooking spray and set aside.
3. In a large bowl, mix together zucchini, sour cream, eggs, ham, and cheese until well combined.
4. In a separate bowl, mix together almond flour, pepper, baking powder, and salt.
5. Mix together wet and dry ingredients until well combined.
6. Pour batter in a prepared muffin tray and bake in preheated oven for 40 minutes.
7. Serve and enjoy.

Nutritional Value (Amount per Serving):

- Calories 148
- Fat 10.8 g

- Carbohydrates 3.6 g
- Sugar 0.7 g
- Protein 9.2 g
- Cholesterol 72 mg

Easy Breakfast Omelet Waffle

Preparation Time: 5 minutes
Cooking Time: 5 minutes
Serve: 1

Ingredients:

- 2 eggs
- 3 tbsp unsweetened almond milk
- 1 tbsp broccoli, chopped
- 1 tbsp red pepper, chopped
- 1 tbsp mozzarella cheese, shredded
- Pepper
- Salt

Directions:

1. Preheat the waffle iron and spray with cooking spray.
2. In a bowl, whisk eggs with almond milk, pepper, and salt.
3. Add remaining ingredients and stir well.
4. Once waffle iron is hot then pour in the egg mixture and cook according to the machine instructions.
5. Serve and enjoy.

Nutritional Value (Amount per Serving):

- Calories 254
- Fat 14.7 g
- Carbohydrates 11 g
- Sugar 6.8 g
- Protein 20.6 g
- Cholesterol 342 mg

Quick & Easy Pancakes

Preparation Time: 5 minutes
Cooking Time: 9 minutes
Serve: 2

Ingredients:

- 2 eggs
- ½ tsp cinnamon
- 1 tsp erythritol
- 2 oz cream cheese

Directions:

1. Add all ingredients into the blender and blend until smooth.
2. Heat pan over medium heat. Spray pan with cooking spray.
3. Pour a ¼ cup of batter into a hot pan and cook for 2 minutes.
4. Turn pancake to other side and cook for 1 minute.
5. Repeat same with remaining batter.
6. Serve with fresh berries and enjoy.

Nutritional Value (Amount per Serving):

- Calories 163
- Fat 14.3 g
- Carbohydrates 1.6 g
- Sugar 0.4 g
- Protein 7.7 g
- Cholesterol 195 mg

Healthy Vegetable Muffins

Preparation Time: 10 minutes
Cooking Time: 25 minutes
Serve: 12

Ingredients:

- 5 eggs, lightly beaten
- 1 cup cheddar cheese, shredded
- ¼ tsp garlic powder
- ½ cup onion, chopped
- ½ cup baby spinach
- 5 oz ham, diced
- 3 cups cauliflower rice, squeeze out excess liquid
- Pepper
- Salt

Directions:

1. Preheat the oven to 375 F/ 190 C.
2. Spray a muffin tray with cooking spray and set aside.
3. In a bowl, whisk eggs with garlic powder, pepper, and salt.
4. Add remaining ingredients and stir to combine.
5. Pour mixture into the prepared muffin tray and bake in preheated oven for 25 minutes.
6. Serve and enjoy.

Nutritional Value (Amount per Serving):

- Calories 103
- Fat 6 g
- Carbohydrates 5 g
- Sugar 2.1 g
- Protein 8.1 g
- Cholesterol 85 mg

Spicy Egg Scrambled

Preparation Time: 10 minutes
Cooking Time: 10 minutes
Serve: 2

Ingredients:

- 4 eggs
- 2 tbsp green onion, sliced
- 2 tbsp fresh parsley, chopped
- 1/3 cup heavy cream
- 1 tomato, diced
- 1 serrano chili pepper, chopped
- 3 tbsp butter
- ¼ tsp pepper
- ½ tsp salt

Directions:

1. Melt butter in a large pan over medium heat.
2. Add tomato and chili and sauté for 1-2 minutes.
3. In a bowl, whisk eggs with cream, parsley, pepper, and salt.
4. Pour egg mixture into the hot pan and stir until egg is scrambled.
5. Garnish with green onion and serve.

Nutritional Value (Amount per Serving):

- Calories 360
- Fat 33.5 g
- Carbohydrates 3.8 g
- Sugar 1.7 g
- Protein 12.2 g
- Cholesterol 401 mg

Crust-less Breakfast Quiche

Preparation Time: 10 minutes
Cooking Time: 55 minutes
Serve: 10

Ingredients:

- 6 eggs
- 5 oz baby spinach
- 7.5 oz cheddar cheese, shredded
- 1 cup heavy cream
- 7.5 oz cream cheese, cut into cube
- 1 lb ground sausage
- Pepper
- Salt

Directions:

1. Preheat the oven to 375 F/ 190 C.
2. Grease casserole dish with butter and set aside.
3. Heat pan over medium-high heat browns the sausage until cooked through.
4. Add cream cheese and stir well with sausage and cook until cheese is melted.
5. Add spinach in microwave safe bowl with 2 tbsp water and microwave for 2-3 minutes.
6. In a bowl, whisk together eggs, pepper, salt, and heavy cream.
7. Add sausage cream cheese mixture in a prepared casserole dish.
8. Add spinach on top of sausage mixture. Sprinkle shredded cheese on top.
9. Now pour egg mixture over spinach and sausage mixture.
10. Place in preheated oven and bake for 35-40 minutes.
11. Remove from oven and allow to cool for 10 minutes.
12. Slice and serve.

Nutritional Value (Amount per Serving):

- Calories 396

- Fat 34.4 g
- Carbohydrates 1.9 g
- Sugar 0.4 g
- Protein 19.7 g
- Cholesterol 198 mg

Scrambled Egg Muffins

Preparation Time: 10 minutes
Cooking Time: 25 minutes
Serve: 12

Ingredients:

- 12 eggs
- ½ cup baby spinach
- 1 cup cheddar cheese, shredded
- ¼ cup mushrooms, diced
- ¼ tsp garlic powder
- 1 cup ham, cooked
- 2 tbsp onion, diced
- 3 tbsp bell pepper, diced
- Pepper
- Salt

Directions:

1. Preheat the oven to 350 F/ 180 C.
2. Spray a muffin tray with cooking spray and set aside.
3. In a large bowl, beat eggs.
4. Add remaining ingredients and mix well.
5. Pour egg mixture in a prepared muffin tray and bake in preheated oven for 20-25 minutes.

Nutritional Value (Amount per Serving):

- Calories 130
- Fat 8.5 g
- Carbohydrates 3.5 g
- Sugar 2 g
- Protein 10.2 g
- Cholesterol 180 mg

Savory Breakfast Casserole

Preparation Time: 10 minutes
Cooking Time: 40 minutes
Serve: 8

Ingredients:

- 12 eggs
- 1 tbsp hot sauce
- ¾ cup heavy cream
- 2 cups cheddar cheese, shredded
- 12 oz breakfast sausage
- Pepper
- Salt

Directions:

1. Preheat the oven to 350 F/ 180 C.
2. Spray casserole dish with cooking spray and set aside.
3. Heat a large pan over medium-high heat.
4. Add sausage to the hot pan and break with a spoon and cook for 5-8 minutes or until meat is no longer pink.
5. Transfer sausage mixture to the prepared casserole dish.
6. In a large bowl, whisk eggs with heavy cream, shredded cheese, and hot sauce.
7. Pour egg mixture over sausage mixture and spread well.
8. Bake in preheated oven for 35-40 minutes.

Nutritional Value (Amount per Serving):

- Calories 391
- Fat 32.2 g
- Carbohydrates 1.2 g
- Sugar 0.7 g
- Protein 23.8 g
- Cholesterol 326 mg

Olive Cheese Omelet

Preparation Time: 5 minutes
Cooking Time: 5 minutes
Serve: 4

Ingredients:

- 4 large eggs
- 1 tsp herb de Provence
- 2 oz cheese
- 8 olives, pitted
- 2 tbsp butter
- 2 tbsp olive oil
- 1/2 tsp salt

Directions:

1. Add eggs, salt, olives, herb de Provence, and olive oil in a large bowl and whisk well until frothy.
2. In a large pan, melt butter over medium heat.
3. Pour egg mixture into the hot pan and spread evenly.
4. Cover pan with a lid and cook for 3 minutes or until omelet lightly golden brown.
5. Turn omelet to other side and cook for 2 minutes more.
6. Serve and enjoy.

Nutritional Value (Amount per Serving):

- Calories 252
- Fat 23 g
- Carbohydrates 1 g
- Sugar 0.5 g
- Protein 10 g
- Cholesterol 216 mg

Cheese Soufflés

Preparation Time: 10 minutes
Cooking Time: 25 minutes
Serve: 8

Ingredients:

- 6 eggs, separated
- 3/4 cup heavy cream
- 1/4 tsp cayenne pepper
- 1/2 tsp xanthan gum
- 1/2 tsp pepper
- 1/4 tsp cream of tartar
- 1/4 cup chives, chopped
- 2 cups cheddar cheese, shredded
- 1 tsp ground mustard
- 1 tsp salt

Directions:

1. Preheat the oven to 350 F/ 180 C.
2. Spray eight ramekins with cooking spray and place on cookie sheet.
3. In a mixing bowl, whisk together almond flour, cayenne pepper, pepper, mustard, salt, and xanthan gum.
4. Slowly add heavy cream and mix until well combined.
5. Whisk in egg yolks, chives, and cheese until well combined.
6. In a large bowl, add egg whites and cream of tartar and beat until stiff peaks form.
7. Gently fold egg white mixture into the almond flour mixture until well combined.
8. Pour mixture into the prepared ramekins and place on cookie sheet.
9. Bake for 25 minutes or until lightly golden brown.
10. Serve and enjoy.

Nutritional Value (Amount per Serving):

- Calories 211

- Fat 17 g
- Carbohydrates 1 g
- Sugar 0.5 g
- Protein 12 g
- Cholesterol 185 mg

Simple Egg Loaf

Preparation Time: 5 minutes
Cooking Time: 30 minutes
Serve: 4

Ingredients:

- 4 eggs
- 4 oz cream cheese
- 4 tbsp butter
- 1 tsp swerve
- 1 tsp vanilla

Directions:

1. Add all ingredients into the small bowl and mix with an electric mixer until well combined and smooth.
2. Spray 9*13-inch baking pan with cooking spray.
3. Pour batter into the prepared pan and bake at 350 F/ 180 C for 30 minutes.
4. Serve and enjoy.

Nutritional Value (Amount per Serving):

- Calories 268
- Fat 25.8 g
- Carbohydrates 1.7 g
- Sugar 0.5 g
- Protein 7.8 g
- Cholesterol 26 mg

Tomato Cheese Omelet

Preparation Time: 10 minutes
Cooking Time: 10 minutes
Serve: 1

Ingredients:

- 3 eggs
- 1 tbsp fresh basil, chopped
- 2 tbsp ricotta cheese, shredded
- 1 tsp butter
- 2 tbsp sun-dried tomatoes, chopped
- 2 tbsp mozzarella cheese, shredded

Directions:

1. Melt butter in a pan over medium heat.
2. Meanwhile, in a bowl, whisk together eggs, sun-dried tomatoes, and basil.
3. Pour egg mixture into the pan.
4. Cover pan with lid and cook over medium-low heat.
5. Mix together mozzarella cheese and ricotta.
6. Remove lid and add mozzarella mixture on top of the omelet.
7. Cover the pan again and cook for 1-2 minutes.
8. Serve and enjoy.

Nutritional Value (Amount per Serving):

- Calories 441
- Fat 31 g
- Carbohydrates 4.9 g
- Sugar 1.7 g
- Protein 36.4 g
- Cholesterol 61 mg

Banana Breakfast Bread

Preparation Time: 10 minutes
Cooking Time: 50 minutes
Serve: 10

Ingredients:

- 3 eggs
- 4 tbsp olive oil
- 1/2 cup walnuts
- 2 cups almond flour
- 3 bananas
- 1 tsp baking soda

Directions:

1. Preheat the oven to 350 F/ 180 C.
2. Spray a loaf pan with cooking spray and set aside.
3. Add all ingredients into the food processor and process until well combined.
4. Pour batter into the loaf pan and bake in preheated oven for 50 minutes.
5. Slices and serve.

Nutritional Value (Amount per Serving):

- Calories 153
- Fat 12 g
- Carbohydrates 9.8 g
- Sugar 4.8 g
- Protein 4 g
- Cholesterol 56 mg

Cheese Bacon Muffins

Preparation Time: 10 minutes
Cooking Time: 20 minutes
Serve: 12

Ingredients:

- 9 eggs
- 8 bacon slices, cooked and chopped
- 3/4 cup heavy cream
- 1 jalapeno pepper, sliced
- 8.5 oz cheddar cheese, shredded
- Pepper
- Salt

Directions:

1. Preheat the oven to 350 F/ 180 C.
2. Spray a muffin tray with cooking spray and add cooked bacon slices to each muffin cup.
3. In a large bowl, whisk together eggs, shredded cheese, cream, pepper, and salt.
4. Pour egg mixture into the prepared muffin cups evenly.
5. Add sliced jalapeno into each muffin cup.
6. Bake for 15-20 minutes.
7. Serve and enjoy.

Nutritional Value (Amount per Serving):

- Calories 236
- Fat 19.1 g
- Carbohydrates 1 g
- Sugar 0.4 g
- Protein 14.9 g
- Cholesterol 19 mg

Mexican Breakfast Frittata

Preparation Time: 10 minutes
Cooking Time: 20 minutes
Serve: 6

Ingredients:

- 8 eggs, scrambled
- 1/2 cup cheddar cheese, grated
- 2 tsp taco seasoning
- 1/2 lb ground beef
- 3 green onion, chopped
- 1/3 lb tomatoes, sliced
- 1 small green pepper, chopped
- 1/2 cup salsa
- 1 tbsp olive oil
- 1/4 tsp salt

Directions:

1. Preheat the oven to 375 F/ 190 C.
2. Heat oil in a pan over medium heat.
3. Add ground meat and sauté until brown.
4. Add salsa and taco seasoning and stir well to coat.
5. Remove meat from the pan and place on a plate.
6. Add green pepper to the pan and cook for a few minutes, until crisp.
7. Return meat to the pan along with green onion and tomato.
8. Add scrambled eggs on top then sprinkle with grated cheese.
9. Bake for 20-25 minutes.
10. Serve and enjoy.

Nutritional Value (Amount per Serving):

- Calories 229
- Fat 13.8 g

- Carbohydrates 4.4 g
- Sugar 2.4 g
- Protein 22 g
- Cholesterol 37 mg

Chapter7: Appetizers & Snacks

Chicken Dip

Preparation Time: 10 minutes
Cooking Time: 25 minutes
Serve: 6

Ingredients:

- 2 cups chicken, cooked and shredded
- 4 tbsp hot sauce
- ½ cup sour cream
- 8 oz cream cheese, softened

Directions:

1. Preheat the oven to 350 F/ 180 C/
2. Add all ingredients in a large bowl and mix until well combined.
3. Transfer mixture in a baking dish and bake in preheated oven for 25 minutes.
4. Serve dip with veggies and enjoy.

Nutritional Value (Amount per Serving):

- Calories 244
- Fat 18.7 g
- Carbohydrates 2 g
- Sugar 0.2 g
- Protein 17 g
- Cholesterol 86 mg

Delicious Crab Dip

Preparation Time: 10 minutes
Cooking Time: 30 minutes
Serve: 8

Ingredients:

- 1 lb crab meat
- ¼ cup mozzarella cheese, shredded
- 1 ½ tbsp old bay seasoning
- ¼ cup parmesan cheese, grated
- 8 oz cream cheese, softened
- ¼ tsp pepper
- ½ tsp salt

Directions:

1. Preheat the oven to 350 F/ 180 C.
2. Add all ingredients except mozzarella cheese in a large bowl and mix until well combined.
3. Transfer bowl mixture to the baking dish and bake in preheated oven for 30 minutes.
4. Remove baking dish from oven and top with mozzarella cheese.
5. Serve with veggies and enjoy.

Nutritional Value (Amount per Serving):

- Calories 171
- Fat 12.2 g
- Carbohydrates 1.8 g
- Sugar 0.1 g
- Protein 11 g
- Cholesterol 66 mg

Healthy Spinach Dip

Preparation Time: 5 minutes
Cooking Time: 5 minutes
Serve: 6

Ingredients:

- 2 tbsp fresh lemon juice
- ¼ cup sour cream
- 1 cup mayonnaise
- ½ tsp onion powder
- ½ tbsp dried dill
- 2 tbsp dried parsley
- 2 oz spinach
- 2 tbsp olive oil
- ¼ tsp pepper
- ½ tsp salt

Directions:

1. Add all ingredients into the bowl and mix until well combined.
2. Serve and enjoy.

Nutritional Value (Amount per Serving):

- Calories 219
- Fat 19.9 g
- Carbohydrates 10.7 g
- Sugar 2.8 g
- Protein 1.1 g
- Cholesterol 14 mg

Chorizo Dip

Preparation Time: 10 minutes
Cooking Time: 10 minutes
Serve: 16

Ingredients:

- 1 lb Monterrey jack cheese, shredded
- 2 tbsp fresh cilantro, chopped
- 2 green onion, sliced
- 2 tbsp pickled jalapenos, diced
- 12 oz chorizo

Directions:

1. Heat large pan over medium heat. Brown chorizo and drain excess grease.
2. In a bowl, mix together chorizo, cilantro, green onion, jalapenos, and cheese.
3. Transfer bowl mixture to the baking dish and bake at 400 F/ 200 C for 10 minutes.
4. Serve and enjoy.

Nutritional Value (Amount per Serving):

- Calories 102
- Fat 8.5 g
- Carbohydrates 0.6 g
- Sugar 0 g
- Protein 5.4 g
- Cholesterol 19 mg

Easy Ranch Dip

Preparation Time: 5 minutes
Cooking Time: 5 minutes
Serve: 8

Ingredients:

- 1 ½ tbsp ranch seasoning
- ½ cup sour cream
- 1 cup mayonnaise

Directions:

1. Add all ingredients in a bowl and mix until well combined.
2. Place in refrigerator for 15 minutes.
3. Serve with veggies and enjoy.

Nutritional Value (Amount per Serving):

- Calories 151
- Fat 12.8 g
- Carbohydrates 7.6 g
- Sugar 1.9 g
- Protein 0.7 g
- Cholesterol 14 mg

Flavorful Seafood Dip

Preparation Time: 10 minutes
Cooking Time: 30 minutes
Serve: 16

Ingredients:

- 4 oz can green chilies
- 2 cups pepper jack cheese, shredded
- 4 oz cream cheese
- ½ tsp old bay seasoning
- 2 garlic cloves, minced
- ½ cup spinach, minced
- 1 onion, minced
- 2 tbsp butter
- 4 oz crab meat
- ½ lb shrimp, cooked

Directions:

1. Preheat the oven to 425 F/ 218 C.
2. Melt butter in large skillet over medium heat.
3. Add garlic and onion to the pan and sauté for 2-3 minutes.
4. Add old bay seasoning and stir for a minute.
5. Add spinach, crab meat, green chilies, and shrimp and cook for 1-2 minutes.
6. Add 1 cup pepper jack cheese and cream cheese and mix well.
7. Top with remaining pepper jack cheese.
8. Place skillet in preheated oven and bake for 20 minutes.

Nutritional Value (Amount per Serving):

- Calories 94
- Fat 6.6 g
- Carbohydrates 1.8 g
- Sugar 0.3 g
- Protein 6.6 g

Tasty Jalapeno Poppers

Preparation Time: 10 minutes
Cooking Time: 20 minutes
Serve: 24

Ingredients:

- 12 jalapeno peppers, cut in half and remove seeds
- 4 oz cheddar cheese, shredded
- 4 oz cream cheese
- 2 oz feta cheese
- ¼ tsp garlic powder
- 1/2 tsp onion powder
- 1/4 cup cilantro, chopped

Directions:

1. Preheat the oven to 425 F/ 218 C.
2. Add all ingredients except jalapeno peppers into the bowl and mix well to combine.
3. Stuff cheese mixture into each jalapeno half and place on a baking tray.
4. Bake for 20 minutes.
5. Serve and enjoy.

Nutritional Value (Amount per Serving):

- Calories 42
- Fat 3.7 g
- Carbohydrates 0.4 g
- Protein 1.9 g
- Sugar 0.2 g
- Cholesterol 12mg

Easy Zucchini Bites

Preparation Time: 10 minutes
Cooking Time: 15 minutes
Serve: 4

Ingredients:

- 1 egg
- 2 cups zucchini, grated
- 1/4 cup cilantro, chopped
- 1/2 cup parmesan cheese, grated
- Pepper
- Salt

Directions:

1. Preheat the oven to 400 F/ 200 C.
2. Spray mini muffin pan with cooking spray and set aside.
3. In a bowl, mix together zucchini, cilantro, cheese, egg, pepper, and salt.
4. Pour mixture into the prepared mini muffin pan and bake for 15 minutes.
5. Serve and enjoy.

Nutritional Value (Amount per Serving):

- Calories 105
- Fat 7.2 g
- Carbohydrates 2 g
- Protein 10.1 g
- Sugar 1.1 g
- Cholesterol 61mg

Cheese Zucchini Nachos

Preparation Time: 10 minutes
Cooking Time: 18 minutes
Serve: 8

Ingredients:

- 1 large zucchini, sliced
- 1 1/2 cups no bean chili
- 2 tbsp olive oil
- 1/2 cup mozzarella cheese, grated
- 3/4 cup cheddar cheese, grated

Directions:

1. Preheat the oven to 350 F/ 175 C.
2. Arrange zucchini slices in greased baking dish.
3. Lightly brush zucchini slices with oil and roast in the oven for 5-8 minutes.
4. Remove zucchini from oven and top with no bean chili, mozzarella cheese, and cheddar cheese.
5. Bake for 10 minutes.
6. Serve and enjoy.

Nutritional Value (Amount per Serving):

- Calories 131
- Fat 9.5 g
- Carbohydrates 4.7 g
- Protein 7.4 g
- Sugar 1.3 g
- Cholesterol 21mg

Zucchini Fries

Preparation Time: 10 minutes
Cooking Time: 20 minutes
Serve: 4

Ingredients:

- 2 eggs
- 1 tbsp heavy cream
- 2 medium zucchinis, peel and cut into matchsticks
- 1/2 cup parmesan cheese, grated
- ¼ tsp garlic powder
- ¼ tsp onion powder
- 1 cup pork rinds

Directions:

1. Preheat the oven to 400 F/ 200 C.
2. In a bowl, whisk together cream and eggs.
3. Add pork rinds in a food processor and process until it looks like breadcrumbs.
4. Add parmesan cheese and process again.
5. Transfer pork rind and parmesan mixture another bowl with onion powder and garlic powder.
6. Dip each zucchini piece into the egg mixture then coat with pork rind and parmesan mixture and place on a baking tray.
7. Bake for 15-20 minutes.

Nutritional Value (Amount per Serving):

- Calories 131
- Fat 8 g
- Carbohydrates 3 g
- Protein 11 g
- Sugar 3 g
- Cholesterol 104mg

Coconut Crackers

Preparation Time: 10 minutes
Cooking Time: 20 minutes
Serve: 9

Ingredients:

- 1 egg
- 1/2 tsp smoked paprika
- 1/2 cup coconut flour
- 2 tbsp butter, softened
- 2 oz cream cheese
- 2 cups cheddar cheese, shredded
- 1/4 tsp garlic powder
- 1/4 tsp onion powder
- 1/4 tsp salt

Directions:

1. Preheat the oven to 350 F/ 180 C.
2. Add all ingredients into the food processor and process until combined.
3. Roll out dough between two parchment paper pieces.
4. Place roll dough sheet on a baking tray and using pizza cutter cut dough into 1-inch squares.
5. Bake in preheated oven for 15 minutes then separate crackers and bake for 5 minutes more.

Nutritional Value (Amount per Serving):

- Calories 157
- Fat 13.7 g
- Carbohydrates 1.2 g
- Protein 7.5 g
- Sugar 0.3 g
- Cholesterol 58mg

Healthy Broccoli Fritters

Preparation Time: 10 minutes
Cooking Time: 10 minutes
Serve: 4

Ingredients:

- 2 eggs, lightly beaten
- 1 cup cheddar cheese, shredded
- 8 oz broccoli florets, chopped
- 1 tbsp olive oil
- 1/2 tsp Cajun seasoning
- 2 tbsp almond flour

Directions:

1. Add all ingredients except oil in a large bowl and mix until well combined.
2. Heat oil in a pan over medium heat.
3. Make patties from mixture and place on a hot pan.
4. Cook patties until lightly browned, about 2-3 minutes on each side.
5. Serve and enjoy.

Nutritional Value (Amount per Serving):

- Calories 194
- Fat 14.2 g
- Carbohydrates 5.3 g
- Protein 12.6 g
- Sugar 1.4 g
- Cholesterol 123mg

Chapter8: Beef, Pork & Lamb

Salsa Beef

Preparation Time: 10 minutes
Cooking Time: 6 hours
Serve: 6

Ingredients:

- 2 lbs beef stew meat, cut into 3/4-inch pieces
- 1 tbsp soy sauce, low-sodium
- 2 cups salsa
- 1/4 cup cilantro, chopped
- 2 garlic cloves, minced
- Pepper
- Salt

Directions:

1. Add all ingredients except cilantro into the slow cooker and stir well.
2. Cover slow cooker with lid and cook on low for 6 hours.
3. Garnish with cilantro and serve.

Nutritional Value (Amount per Serving):

- Calories 307
- Fat 9.6 g
- Carbohydrates 5.8 g
- Sugar 2.7 g
- Protein 47.4 g
- Cholesterol 135 mg

Parmesan Pork Chops

Preparation Time: 10 minutes
Cooking Time: 20 minutes
Serve: 6

Ingredients:

- 6 pork chops, boneless
- 1 1/2 cups parmesan cheese, grated
- 4 tbsp Dijon mustard
- 3 tbsp olive oil
- 1/2 tsp basil, dried
- 1/2 tsp oregano, dried
- 1/2 tsp thyme
- 1/2 tsp garlic powder
- 1/2 tsp pepper
- 1/2 tsp onion powder
- 1/2 tsp salt

Directions:

1. In a small bowl, mix together basil, oregano, onion powder, thyme, garlic powder, olive oil, mustard, 1/4 tsp pepper, and 1/4 tsp salt.
2. Add pork chops in a large bowl.
3. Pour marinade over pork chops and mix well until combined.
4. Place in refrigerator for overnight.
5. Preheat the oven at 400 F/ 200 C.
6. Place parmesan cheese in a shallow dish.
7. Coat each pork chop with cheese.
8. Place coated pork chops on a baking tray. Season with pepper and salt.
9. Bake for 20 minutes.
10. Serve and enjoy.

Nutritional Value (Amount per Serving):

- Calories 327
- Fat 27.4 g
- Carbohydrates 1.3 g
- Sugar 0 g
- Protein 18.7 g
- Cholesterol 69 mg

Greek Pork Chops

Preparation Time: 10 minutes
Cooking Time: 35 minutes
Serve: 4

Ingredients:

- 4 pork loin chops, boneless
- 1 tbsp fresh rosemary, chopped
- 2 garlic cloves, minced
- 1/4 tsp black pepper
- 1/2 tsp kosher salt

Directions:

1. Season pork chops with pepper and salt.
2. In a small bowl, mix together garlic and rosemary.
3. Rub garlic and rosemary mixture on each pork chops.
4. Place pork chops on a roasting pan and roast in an oven for 10 minutes at 425 F/ 218 C.
5. Turn temperature to 350 F/ 175 C and continue roasting for about 25 minutes.
6. Serve and enjoy.

Nutritional Value (Amount per Serving):

- Calories 262
- Fat 20 g
- Carbohydrates 1.4 g
- Sugar 0 g
- Protein 18.2 g
- Cholesterol 69 mg

Meatloaf

Preparation Time: 10 minutes
Cooking Time: 60 minutes
Serve: 8

Ingredients:

- 2 large eggs
- 1 small onion, chopped
- 1/2 cup parmesan cheese, grated
- 2 lbs ground beef
- 1 tsp garlic powder
- 1/4 tsp pepper
- 2 tsp salt

Directions:

1. In mixing bowl, add all ingredients and mix well until combined.
2. Spray loaf pan with cooking spray.
3. Add beef mixture into the loaf pan and bake at 350 F/ 180 C for 60 minutes.
4. Allow to cool completely.
5. Slice and serve.

Nutritional Value (Amount per Serving):

- Calories 233
- Fat 8.3 g
- Carbohydrates 1.2 g
- Sugar 0.6 g
- Protein 36.1 g
- Cholesterol 148 mg

Beef Stir Fry

Preparation Time: 10 minutes
Cooking Time: 10 minutes
Serve: 4

Ingredients:

- 1 lb beef, cut into slices
- 3 cups broccoli florets
- 1/2 tsp Dijon mustard
- 1 tsp garlic, minced
- 1 tsp sesame oil
- 2 tbsp water
- 2 tbsp soy sauce
- 1 tsp olive oil
- 3 scallions, chopped
- 1/2 cup parsley, chopped
- 2 red peppers, sliced
- 1 tsp ginger

Directions:

1. In mixing bowl, add beef slices, mustard, ginger, garlic, oil, water and soy sauce. Mix well and set aside.
2. Heat olive oil in a pan over high heat.
3. Add pepper and broccoli and cook until tender.
4. Add beef mixture and cook until meat is cooked.
5. Add parsley and scallions. Stir well.

Nutritional Value (Amount per Serving):

- Calories 277
- Fat 9.9 g
- Carbohydrates 9.0 g
- Sugar 2.8 g
- Protein 37.8 g

Lamb Kebabs

Preparation Time: 10 minutes
Cooking Time: 10 minutes
Serve: 6

Ingredients:
- 1 1/2 lbs lamb, cut into 2-inch pieces
- 1/2 tsp black pepper
- 5 garlic cloves, minced
- 2 tsp oregano, chopped
- 1 1/2 tbsp parsley, chopped
- 1 1/2 tbsp mint, chopped
- 1 1/2 tbsp rosemary, chopped
- 5 tbsp olive oil
- 1/8 tsp red pepper flakes
- 1 lemon zest
- 1 tsp kosher salt

Directions:
1. In a mixing bowl, combine together olive oil, red pepper flakes, lemon zest, pepper, salt, garlic, oregano, parsley, mint, and rosemary.
2. Add lamb pieces into the bowl and mix well and place in the refrigerator for 2 hours.
3. Preheat the grill medium-high heat.
4. Thread the lamb chunks onto skewers and grill for 10 minutes. Turn once.

Nutritional Value (Amount per Serving):
- Calories 320
- Fat 20.2 g
- Carbohydrates 2 g
- Sugar 0.1 g
- Protein 32.2 g
- Cholesterol 102 mg

Lamb Meatloaf

Preparation Time: 10 minutes
Cooking Time: 45 minutes
Serve: 6

Ingredients:

- 1 1/2 lbs ground lamb
- 3 garlic cloves, minced
- 2 tbsp balsamic vinegar
- 2 large eggs
- 1 tbsp fresh rosemary
- 1/2 cup sun-dried tomatoes, chopped
- 2 onion, chopped
- Pepper
- Salt

Directions:

1. Preheat the oven 375 F/ 190 C.
2. Spray a loaf pan with cooking spray and set aside.
3. In a bowl, whisk together eggs, salt, pepper, and vinegar.
4. Add rosemary, sun-dried tomatoes, onion, and garlic and mix well.
5. Add lamb and mix just until combined.
6. Pour meatloaf mixture into the prepared pan and bake for 40-45 minutes.
7. Slice and serve.

Nutritional Value (Amount per Serving):

- Calories 253
- Fat 10.1 g
- Carbohydrates 4 g
- Sugar 1.1 g
- Protein 34.6 g
- Cholesterol 164 mg

Pork Roast

Preparation Time: 10 minutes
Cooking Time: 1 hour 30 minutes
Serve: 6

Ingredients:

- 3 lbs pork roast, boneless
- 1 cup of water
- 1 onion, chopped
- 3 garlic cloves, chopped
- 1 tbsp black pepper
- 1 rosemary sprig
- 2 fresh oregano sprigs
- 2 fresh thyme sprigs
- 1 tbsp olive oil
- 1 tbsp kosher salt

Directions:

1. Preheat the oven to 350 F/ 180 C.
2. Season pork roast with pepper and salt.
3. Heat olive oil in a stockpot and sear pork roast on each side, about 4 minutes or until lightly golden brown.
4. Add onion and garlic. Pour in the water, oregano, and thyme and bring to boil for a minute.
5. Cover pot and roast in the preheated oven for 1 1/2 hours.

Nutritional Value (Amount per Serving):

- Calories 502
- Fat 23.8 g
- Carbohydrates 2.9 g
- Sugar 0.8 g
- Protein 65.1 g
- Cholesterol 195 mg

Garlic Olive Pork Chops

Preparation Time: 10 minutes
Cooking Time: 30 minutes
Serve: 6

Ingredients:

- 6 pork chops, boneless and cut into thick slices
- 1/4 cup chicken stock
- 2 garlic cloves, chopped
- 1 large onion, sliced
- 8 oz ragu
- 1 tbsp olive oil
- 1/8 tsp ground cinnamon
- 1/2 cup olives, pitted and sliced

Directions:

1. Heat olive oil in a pan over medium-high heat.
2. Place pork chops in a pan and cook until lightly brown and set aside.
3. Cook garlic and onion in the same pan over medium heat, until onion is softened.
4. Add stock and bring to boil over high heat.
5. Return pork to pan and stir in ragu and remaining ingredients.
6. Cover and simmer for 20 minutes.
7. Serve and enjoy.

Nutritional Value (Amount per Serving):

- Calories 321
- Fat 23.5 g
- Carbohydrates 7.2 g
- Sugar 1.1 g
- Protein 19 g
- Cholesterol 69 mg

Roasted Beef

Preparation Time: 10 minutes
Cooking Time: 30 minutes
Serve: 6

Ingredients:

- 2 lbs sirloin steak, cut into 1-inch pieces
- 3 tbsp fresh lemon juice
- 1 tsp dried oregano
- 1/4 cup water
- 1/4 cup olive oil
- 2 garlic cloves, minced
- 1 1/2 cups fresh parsley, chopped
- 1/2 tsp black pepper
- 1 tsp salt

Directions:

1. Add all ingredients except beef into the large bowl and mix well together.
2. Pour bowl mixture into the large zip-lock bag.
3. Add beef into the bag and shake well and refrigerate for 1 hour.
4. Preheat the oven 400 F/ 200 C.
5. Place marinated beef on a baking tray and bake for 30 minutes.
6. Serve and enjoy.

Nutritional Value (Amount per Serving):

- Calories 365
- Fat 18.1 g
- Carbohydrates 2 g
- Sugar 0.4 g
- Protein 46.6 g
- Cholesterol 135 mg

Coconut Pork Curry

Preparation Time: 15 minutes
Cooking Time: 4 hours 20 minutes
Serve: 8

Ingredients:

- 4 lbs pork shoulder, boneless and cut into pieces
- 2 tbsp olive oil
- 3 cups chicken stock
- 1 cup unsweetened coconut milk
- 14 oz can tomato, diced
- 3 tbsp fresh ginger, minced
- 3 garlic cloves, minced
- 1 large onion, chopped
- 1/2 tsp ground turmeric
- 1 tbsp ground cumin
- 1 tbsp curry powder

Directions:

1. Heat oil in a pan over medium heat.
2. Season pork with pepper and salt,
3. Add pork to the pan and brown them on all sides.
4. Transfer pork into the slow cooker.
5. Add onion, turmeric, cumin, curry powder, ginger, and garlic to the pan and sauté for 5 minutes.
6. Transfer pan mixture into the slow cooker.
7. Add coconut milk and tomatoes into the slow cooker and stir well.
8. Cover slow cooker with lid and cook on high for 4 hours.
9. Stir well and serve.

Nutritional Value (Amount per Serving):

- Calories 798

- Fat 59.8 g
- Carbohydrates 8.9 g
- Sugar 3.9 g
- Protein 54.9 g
- Cholesterol 204 mg

Asian Beef Stew

Preparation Time: 10 minutes
Cooking Time: 5 hours 10 minutes
Serve: 8

Ingredients:

- 3 lbs beef stew meat, trimmed
- 1/2 cup Thai red curry paste
- 1/3 cup tomato paste
- 14 oz can unsweetened coconut milk
- 2 tsp ginger, minced
- 2 garlic cloves, minced
- 1 medium onion, sliced
- 2 cups carrots, julienned
- 2 cups broccoli florets
- 2 tsp fresh lime juice
- 2 tbsp fish sauce
- 2 tbsp olive oil
- 2 tsp sea salt

Directions:

1. Heat 1 tbsp oil in a pan over medium-high heat.
2. Add meat in the hot pan and brown the meat on all sides.
3. Transfer brown meat to slow cooker.
4. Add remaining oil in a pan and sauté ginger, garlic, and onion over medium-high heat for 5 minutes.
5. Add coconut milk and stir well.
6. Transfer pan mixture to the slow cooker.
7. Add remaining ingredients except for carrots and broccoli into the slow cooker.
8. Cover slow cooker and cook on high for 5 hours.
9. Add carrots and broccoli during the last 30 minutes cooking.
10. Serve and enjoy.

Nutritional Value (Amount per Serving):

- Calories 524
- Fat 27.4 g
- Carbohydrates 12.4 g
- Sugar 5 g
- Protein 54 g
- Cholesterol 152 mg

Chapter9: Poultry

Baked Chicken

Preparation Time: 10 minutes
Cooking Time: 30 minutes
Serve: 4

Ingredients:

- 2 lbs chicken tenders
- 1 cup cherry tomatoes
- 2 tbsp olive oil
- 3 dill sprigs
- 1 large zucchini
- For topping:
- 2 tbsp feta cheese, crumbled
- 1 tbsp fresh dill, chopped
- 1 tbsp olive oil
- 1 tbsp fresh lemon juice

Directions:

1. Preheat the oven to 400 F/ 200 C.
2. Drizzle the olive oil on a baking tray then place chicken, zucchini, dill, and tomatoes on the tray. Season with salt.
3. Bake chicken for 30 minutes.
4. Meanwhile, in a small bowl, stir together all topping ingredients.
5. Place chicken on the serving tray then top with veggies and remove dill sprigs.
6. Sprinkle topping mixture on top of chicken and vegetables.
7. Serve and enjoy.

Nutritional Value (Amount per Serving):

- Calories 557

- Fat 28.6 g
- Carbohydrates 5.2 g
- Sugar 2.9 g
- Protein 67.9 g
- Cholesterol 206 mg

Herb Marinated Chicken

Preparation Time: 10 minutes
Cooking Time: 15 minutes
Serve: 4

Ingredients:

- 1 lb chicken breasts, skinless and boneless
- 1/2 tsp cumin
- 1 tsp dried oregano
- 1 tbsp lemon juice
- 1 tbsp balsamic vinegar
- 2 garlic cloves, minced
- 1/4 tsp paprika
- 1/2 tsp onion powder
- 1/2 tsp dried basil
- 3 tbsp olive oil
- 1/2 tsp salt

Directions:

1. Add all ingredients except chicken into the zip-lock bag and mix well.
2. Add chicken into the bag and shake well to coat.
3. Place marinated chicken in the fridge for 8 hours.
4. Preheat the grill over medium heat.
5. Remove chicken from marinade and place on a hot grill and grill for 6-7 minutes per side.

Nutritional Value (Amount per Serving):

- Calories 314
- Fat 19.1 g
- Carbohydrates 1.5 g
- Sugar 0.3 g
- Protein 33.1 g
- Cholesterol 101 mg

Chicken Thighs

Preparation Time: 10 minutes
Cooking Time: 60 minutes
Serve: 6

Ingredients:

- 8 chicken thighs
- 1/4 cup capers, drained
- 10 oz roasted red peppers, drained and sliced
- 2 cups grape tomatoes
- 1 tbsp olive oil
- 3 tbsp parsley, chopped
- 1 tsp dried oregano
- 6 garlic cloves, peeled and crushed
- Pepper
- Salt

Directions:

1. Preheat the oven to 400 F/ 200 C.
2. Season chicken with pepper and salt.
3. Heat olive oil in a pan over medium-high heat.
4. Sear chicken in a hot pan until lightly golden brown from all the sides.
5. Remove chicken from heat. Stir in oregano, garlic, capers, red peppers, and tomatoes.
6. Season with pepper and salt and spread on a baking tray.
7. Roast in for 45-50 minutes.
8. Garnish with parsley and serve.

Nutritional Value (Amount per Serving):

- Calories 422
- Fat 17.1 g
- Carbohydrates 7.1 g

- Sugar 3.7 g
- Protein 57.8 g
- Cholesterol 173 mg

Balsamic Chicken

Preparation Time: 10 minutes
Cooking Time: 15 minutes
Serve: 4

Ingredients:
- 1 1/2 lbs chicken thighs
- 1/2 tsp dried oregano
- 1 1/2 cup marinated artichokes
- 2 cups cherry tomatoes
- 6 fresh basil leaves
- 3 tbsp balsamic vinegar
- 1/4 tsp dried thyme
- 1/4 tsp black pepper
- 1/2 tsp salt

Directions:
1. Spray a large skillet with cooking spray and heat over medium-high heat.
2. Sear chicken in a hot skillet for 3-4 minutes on each side.
3. Add tomatoes, marinated artichokes, balsamic vinegar, and seasoning in a chicken skillet.
4. Turn heat to medium. Cover and simmer for 10 minutes.
5. Turn heat to high and cook until all liquid evaporates.
6. Turn chicken occasionally and cook until chicken is lightly browned or until cooked.
7. Remove from heat and garnish with fresh basil and serve.

Nutritional Value (Amount per Serving):
- Calories 398
- Fat 17.3 g
- Carbohydrates 6.4 g
- Sugar 2.9 g
- Protein 50.6 g

Grilled Chicken

Preparation Time: 10 minutes
Cooking Time: 12 minutes
Serve: 4

Ingredients:

- 2 lbs chicken breasts
- 6 tbsp fresh parsley, chopped
- 6 tbsp olive oil
- 6 tbsp fresh lemon juice
- 1 1/2 tsp dried oregano
- 1 tsp paprika
- 4 garlic cloves, minced
- Pepper
- Salt

Directions:

1. Add lemon juice, oregano, paprika, garlic, parsley, and olive oil to a large zip-lock bag.
2. Pierce chicken with fork and season with pepper and salt.
3. Add chicken into the zip-lock bag and marinate for 20 minutes.
4. Preheat the grill over medium-high heat.
5. Grill marinated chicken for 4-6 minutes per side or until cooked.
6. Serve and enjoy.

Nutritional Value (Amount per Serving):

- Calories 627
- Fat 38.2 g
- Carbohydrates 2.8 g
- Sugar 0.6 g
- Protein 66.3 g
- Cholesterol 202 mg

Lemon Butter Chicken Piccata

Preparation Time: 10 minutes
Cooking Time: 15 minutes
Serve: 4

Ingredients:

- 8 chicken thighs, skinless and boneless
- 1 thyme sprig
- 3 garlic cloves, crushed
- 2 tbsp capers, drained
- 1/2 cup dry white wine
- 2 tbsp fresh parsley, chopped
- 1 tbsp butter
- 1 1/2 tbsp fresh lemon juice
- 3/4 cup chicken stock
- 3 tbsp olive oil
- 1/4 tsp black pepper
- 1/2 tsp kosher salt

Directions:

1. Season chicken with pepper and salt.
2. Heat 1 tbsp of oil in a pan over medium-high heat.
3. Add chicken to the pan and cook for 5 minutes.
4. Turn chicken to another side.
5. Add thyme, garlic, capers, and wine and cook for 2 minutes.
6. Add stock and remaining oil to the pan. Bring to boil.
7. Turn heat to medium and cook for 8 minutes.
8. Remove pan from heat. Add butter and lemon juice. Stir well.
9. Garnish with parsley and serve.

Nutritional Value (Amount per Serving):

- Calories 703

- Fat 35.3 g
- Carbohydrates 2.2 g
- Sugar 0.5 g
- Protein 85 g
- Cholesterol 48 mg

Chicken Avocado Salad

Preparation Time: 10 minutes
Cooking Time: 10 minutes
Serve: 4

Ingredients:

- 2 chicken breasts, cooked and chopped
- 4 bacon slices, cooked and chopped
- 1 cup celery, diced
- 2 avocado, chopped
- 3 tbsp olive oil
- 3 tbsp fresh lemon juice
- 1 tsp dried dill
- 1 tbsp dried chives
- 1/2 tsp black pepper
- 1 tsp salt

Directions:

1. Add all ingredients large mixing bowl and toss well to combine.
2. Serve and enjoy.

Nutritional Value (Amount per Serving):

- Calories 545
- Fat 43.6 g
- Carbohydrates 10.2 g
- Sugar 1.1 g
- Protein 30.4 g
- Cholesterol 94 mg

Chicken Curried Salad

Preparation Time: 10 minutes
Cooking Time: 10 minutes
Serve: 4

Ingredients:

- 8 oz chicken, cooked and diced
- 2 oz walnuts, chopped
- 2 tbsp green onion, chopped
- For dressing:
- 1 tsp curry powder
- 1 tbsp lemon juice
- 2 tbsp fresh cilantro, chopped
- 1/8 tsp cayenne
- 1/2 cup mayonnaise
- 1/4 tsp pepper
- 1/4 tsp salt

Directions:

1. In a small bowl, mix together all dressing ingredients and set aside.
2. Add walnuts, green onion, and chicken into the large mixing bowl and mix well.
3. Pour dressing over salad and toss well to coat.
4. Serve and enjoy.

Nutritional Value (Amount per Serving):

- Calories 372
- Fat 31.5 g
- Carbohydrates 2.4 g
- Sugar 0.5 g
- Protein 18.6 g
- Cholesterol 42 mg

Paprika Chicken

Preparation Time: 10 minutes
Cooking Time: 35 minutes
Serve: 4

Ingredients:

- 4 chicken breasts, skinless and boneless, cut into chunks
- 2 tbsp smoked paprika
- 3 tbsp olive oil
- 1 1/2 tsp garlic, minced
- 2 tbsp lemon juice
- Pepper
- Salt

Directions:

1. Preheat the oven to 350 F/ 180 C.
2. In a small bowl, mix together garlic, lemon juice, paprika, and olive oil.
3. Season chicken with pepper and salt.
4. Spread 1/3 bowl mixture on the bottom of the casserole dish.
5. Add seasoned chicken into the casserole dish and rub with dish sauce.
6. Pour remaining sauce on top of the chicken and rub well.
7. Bake for 30-35 minutes.
8. Serve and enjoy.

Nutritional Value (Amount per Serving):

- Calories 381
- Fat 21.8 g
- Carbohydrates 2.6 g
- Sugar 0.5 g
- Protein 42.9 g
- Cholesterol 34 mg

Creamy Chicken Basil Salad

Preparation Time: 10 minutes
Cooking Time: 5 minutes
Serve: 1

Ingredients:

- 1 cup chicken breast, cooked and shredded
- 1 tsp vinegar
- 1 tbsp sour cream
- 2 tsp fresh basil, chopped
- 1/4 cup cucumber, diced
- Pepper
- Salt

Directions:

1. Add all ingredients into the mixing bowl and toss well to combine.
2. Season salad with pepper and salt.
3. Place in refrigerator for 10 minutes.
4. Serve and enjoy.

Nutritional Value (Amount per Serving):

- Calories 243
- Fat 6.8 g
- Carbohydrates 1.6 g
- Sugar 0.5 g
- Protein 41.2 g
- Cholesterol 36 mg

Chapter 10: Seafood

Shrimp Salad

Preparation Time: 10 minutes
Cooking Time: 10 minutes
Serve: 8

Ingredients:

- 4 oz feta cheese, crumbled
- 2 cups baby spinach leaves
- 4 1/2 cup romaine lettuce leaves
- 1 lb shrimp, peeled and deveined
- 1/2 cup Italian dressing
- 1 tomato, chopped
- 1 cucumber, peeled and chopped

Directions:

1. Add shrimp in a baking dish and pour 1/4 cup Italian dressing over shrimp and place dish in the fridge for 30 minutes.
2. Remove shrimp from marinade and grill for 5 minutes.
3. Add remaining ingredients into the large mixing bowl.
4. Add grill shrimp into the bowl and toss well.
5. Serve and enjoy.

Nutritional Value (Amount per Serving):

- Calories 183
- Fat 10.4 g
- Carbohydrates 6.7 g
- Sugar 3.6 g
- Protein 15.7 g
- Cholesterol 147 mg

Sautéed Shrimp with Cheese

Preparation Time: 10 minutes
Cooking Time: 15 minutes
Serve: 6

Ingredients:

- 1 lb shrimp, peeled and deveined
- 2 tbsp capers, rinsed and drained
- 1 tbsp oregano
- 15 oz can tomato, diced
- 2 cups fennel bulb, cut into strips
- 1 tbsp olive oil
- 1/4 cup feta cheese, crumbled
- 1/4 tsp black pepper

Directions:

1. Heat oil in a pan over medium heat.
2. Add fennel in a pan and cook until lightly brown for 6-8 minutes.
3. Add oregano and tomatoes and cook for 30 seconds.
4. Add shrimp and stir until it turns to pink and just cooked through, about 5 minutes.
5. Stir in pepper and capers.
6. Sprinkled with cheese and serve.

Nutritional Value (Amount per Serving):

- Calories 154
- Fat 5.1 g
- Carbohydrates 7.8 g
- Sugar 2.7 g
- Protein 19.3 g
- Cholesterol 165 mg

Easy Shrimp Skewers

Preparation Time: 10 minutes
Cooking Time: 10 minutes
Serve: 6

Ingredients:

- 1 1/2 lbs shrimp, deveined
- 2 fresh lemon juice
- 1/2 tbsp dried oregano
- 2 tsp garlic paste
- 1/4 cup olive oil
- 1 tsp sweet paprika
- Pepper
- Salt

Directions:

1. Add all ingredients into the large bowl and toss well.
2. Cover bowl and place in the refrigerator for 1 hour.
3. Thread 2-3 marinated shrimp on each skewer and grill for 5-7 minutes. Turn halfway through.
4. Serve and enjoy.

Nutritional Value (Amount per Serving):

- Calories 172
- Fat 8.7 g
- Carbohydrates 3.4 g
- Sugar 0.4 g
- Protein 21.6 g
- Cholesterol 162 mg

Lemon Butter Scallops

Preparation Time: 10 minutes
Cooking Time: 10 minutes
Serve: 2

Ingredients:

- 8 large sea scallops, removed side muscle
- 1 tbsp olive oil
- Pepper
- Salt
- For lemon butter:
- 2 tbsp fresh parsley, minced
- 2 tbsp butter
- 1/2 lemon juice
- 1 garlic cloves, minced

Directions:

1. Season scallops with pepper and salt.
2. Heat olive oil in a pan over medium-high heat.
3. Add scallops to a pan and sear for 2 minutes per side or until lightly golden brown.
4. Remove scallops from pan and set aside.
5. Add parsley, lemon, garlic, and butter to the pan and stir until butter melted.
6. Return scallops to the pan and cooks for a minute per side.
7. Serve and enjoy.

Nutritional Value (Amount per Serving):

- Calories 276
- Fat 19.6 g
- Carbohydrates 4.4 g
- Sugar 0.3 g
- Protein 20.7 g
- Cholesterol 70 mg

Delicious Fish Stew

Preparation Time: 10 minutes
Cooking Time: 30 minutes
Serve: 5

Ingredients:

- 14 oz white fish, cut into chunks
- 1 1/4 cup chicken stock
- 14 oz plum tomatoes
- 2 tbsp olive oil
- 1/4 cup fennel bulb, halved and shredded
- 2 garlic cloves, sliced
- 1/4 cup parsley, chopped
- 8.5 oz prawns, peeled and cooked
- 1/2 cup white wine
- 1 tsp paprika
- 1/8 tsp red pepper flakes

Directions:

1. Heat olive oil in a saucepan over medium heat.
2. Add garlic into the pan and sauté for 2 minutes.
3. Add fennel and cook for 5 minutes or until softened.
4. Add paprika and red pepper flakes. Stir well.
5. Add wine and simmer until almost gone.
6. Add stock and tomatoes and simmer for 15-20 minutes.
7. Add white fish chunks and cook for 3 minutes.
8. Add prawns and stir for minutes.
9. Garnish with parsley and serve.

Nutritional Value (Amount per Serving):

- Calories 387
- Fat 28.7 g

- Carbohydrates 6.8 g
- Sugar 3.6 g
- Protein 22.7 g
- Cholesterol 105 mg

Shrimp Dinner

Preparation Time: 10 minutes
Cooking Time: 28 minutes
Serve: 8

Ingredients:

- 2 lbs shrimp, peeled and deveined
- 3 tbsp olive oil
- 1/2 cup olives, halved
- 1/4 cup shallots, sliced
- 2 fennel bulbs, cut into wedges
- 2 tbsp parsley, chopped
- 4 oz feta cheese, crumbled
- 1 tsp lemon zest, grated
- 2 tsp dried oregano
- Pepper
- Salt

Directions:

1. Preheat the oven 450 F/ 232 C.
2. Toss 2 tbsp oil, olives, garlic, shallots, fennel, pepper, and salt together in a bowl.
3. Spread vegetable mixture on a baking tray and roast for 20 minutes.
4. Toss shrimp, 1 tbsp oil, lemon zest, oregano, pepper and salt in a bowl.
5. Spread feta cheese and shrimp over roasted veggies and roast for 6-8 minutes.
6. Garnish with parsley and serve.

Nutritional Value (Amount per Serving):

- Calories 249
- Fat 11.3 g
- Carbohydrates 7.9 g
- Sugar 0.7 g

- Protein 28.8 g
- Cholesterol 251 mg

Spicy Salmon

Preparation Time: 10 minutes
Cooking Time: 10 minutes
Serve: 4

Ingredients:

- 20 oz salmon fillets
- 1/2 tsp paprika
- 1 tsp cumin
- 1/4 tsp black pepper
- 1/4 cup parsley, chopped
- 8 lemon wedges
- 1/2 tsp kosher salt

Directions:

1. In a small bowl, combine together paprika, cumin, pepper, and salt.
2. Spray pan with cooking spray.
3. Place salmon fillet to the pan and evenly coat with spice mixture.
4. Place lemon wedges on the edge of the pan.
5. Broil salmon on high for 8-10 minutes.
6. Garnish with parsley and serve.

Nutritional Value (Amount per Serving):

- Calories 196
- Fat 9 g
- Carbohydrates 2 g
- Sugar 0.7 g
- Protein 27.9 g
- Cholesterol 63 mg

Shrimp Cilantro Salad

Preparation Time: 10 minutes
Cooking Time: 10 minutes
Serve: 4

Ingredients:

- 1 lb medium shrimp, peeled, deveined, and cooked
- 2 eggs, hard-boiled and chopped
- 1/2 green bell pepper, chopped
- 2 celery stalks, diced
- 2 radishes, diced
- 1/2 onion, diced
- 2 tbsp fresh lime juice
- 1 jalapeno pepper, chopped
- 4 tbsp mayonnaise
- Salt

Directions:

1. Add all ingredients into the large mixing bowl and toss well to combine.
2. Serve immediately and enjoy.

Nutritional Value (Amount per Serving):

- Calories 210
- Fat 8.5 g
- Carbohydrates 6.6 g
- Sugar 2.7 g
- Protein 27.6 g
- Cholesterol 308 mg

Tuna Salad

Preparation Time: 10 minutes
Cooking Time: 5 minutes
Serve: 2

Ingredients:

- 2 cans of tuna water packed
- 1/2 cucumber, peeled and chopped
- 1/4 small onion, chopped
- 1 celery stalk, chopped
- 1/2 fresh lime juice
- 1/3 cup mayonnaise
- Pepper
- Salt

Directions:

1. Add all ingredients into the mixing bowl and mix until well combined.
2. Serve and enjoy.

Nutritional Value (Amount per Serving):

- Calories 389
- Fat 18.3 g
- Carbohydrates 13.2 g
- Sugar 4.3 g
- Protein 41.6 g
- Cholesterol 82 mg

Tasty Seasoned Shrimp

Preparation Time: 5 minutes
Cooking Time: 10 minutes
Serve: 4

Ingredients:

- 32 oz shrimp, peeled and deveined
- 2 tbsp old bay seasoning
- 1 tbsp olive oil
- 1/2 fresh lemon juice

Directions:

1. Add all ingredients into the large bowl and toss until well coated.
2. Heat large pan over medium-high heat.
3. Add shrimp into the pan and cook for 2 minutes on each side.
4. Serve and enjoy.

Nutritional Value (Amount per Serving):

- Calories 301
- Fat 7.4 g
- Carbohydrates 3.6 g
- Sugar 0.1 g
- Protein 51.7 g
- Cholesterol 478 mg

Chapter 11: Soup & Sides

Tasty Chicken Soup

Preparation Time: 10 minutes
Cooking Time: 30 minutes
Serve: 4

Ingredients:

- 1 lb chicken breast
- ½ cup heavy cream
- 8 oz cream cheese
- ½ tbsp taco seasoning
- 10 oz can tomato
- 1 tbsp olive oil
- 3 cups chicken stock
- Salt

Directions:

1. Heat oil in a pot over medium heat.
2. Add tomatoes and taco seasoning to the pot and cook for 1 minute.
3. Add stock and chicken. Cover pot and simmer for 25 minutes.
4. Remove chicken from pot and shred using a fork and set aside.
5. Stir the heavy cream and cream cheese in the soup.
6. Puree the soup using an immersion blender until smooth.
7. Once the chicken is melted then return shredded chicken to the pot and stir well.
8. Season soup with salt and serve.

Nutritional Value (Amount per Serving):

- Calories 439
- Fat 32.1 g
- Carbohydrates 7.6 g

- Sugar 3.4 g
- Protein 29.8 g
- Cholesterol 156 mg

Spinach Soup

Preparation Time: 10 minutes
Cooking Time: 15 minutes
Serve: 2

Ingredients:

- 5.5 oz spinach
- 1 tbsp butter
- 10 oz water
- 1 chicken stock cube
- 2 garlic cloves, chopped
- 1 small onion, chopped
- 3.5 oz heavy cream
- Pepper
- Salt

Directions:

1. Melt butter in a saucepan over medium heat.
2. Add onion and sauté until onion is softened.
3. Add garlic and sauté for a minute.
4. Add half water, stock cube, and spinach and stir well.
5. Cover the saucepan with a lid and cook until spinach is wilted.
6. Remove saucepan from heat.
7. Puree the soup using an immersion blender until smooth.
8. Add remaining water and cream and stir well.
9. Season soup with pepper and salt.
10. Serve and enjoy.

Nutritional Value (Amount per Serving):

- Calories 263
- Fat 24.6 g
- Carbohydrates 9.1 g

- Sugar 1.9 g
- Protein 4.3 g
- Cholesterol 84 mg

Broccoli Cheese Soup

Preparation Time: 10 minutes
Cooking Time: 15 minutes
Serve: 6

Ingredients:

- 8 oz broccoli florets
- 3 tbsp almonds, chopped
- 10 oz goat cheese
- ½ cup heavy cream
- 3 cups chicken stock
- 1 tsp salt

Directions:

1. In a large saucepan, mix together stock, cheese, broccoli, and heavy cream. Bring mixture to boil.
2. Turn heat to low and simmer for 15 minutes.
3. Remove pan from heat. Puree the soup using blender until smooth.
4. Garnish with almonds and serve.

Nutritional Value (Amount per Serving):

- Calories 283
- Fat 22.4 g
- Carbohydrates 4.8 g
- Sugar 2.2 g
- Protein 16.7 g
- Cholesterol 63 mg

Roasted Parmesan Cauliflower

Preparation Time: 10 minutes
Cooking Time: 25 minutes
Serve: 4

Ingredients:

- 8 cups cauliflower florets
- 3/4 tsp dried marjoram
- 2 tbsp olive oil
- 1/2 cup parmesan cheese, shredded
- 2 tbsp balsamic vinegar
- 1/4 tsp black pepper
- 1/4 tsp salt

Directions:

1. Preheat the oven to 450 F/ 232 C.
2. In a large bowl, toss cauliflower florets with pepper, marjoram, oil, and salt.
3. Spread cauliflower florets on a baking tray and bake in preheated oven for 15-20 minutes.
4. Drizzle cauliflower florets with vinegar and sprinkle with shredded cheese.
5. Return cauliflower florets into the oven for 5 minutes or until cheese is melted.
6. Serve and enjoy.

Nutritional Value (Amount per Serving):

- Calories 154
- Fat 9.9 g
- Carbohydrates 11.2 g
- Sugar 4.8 g
- Protein 7.8 g
- Cholesterol 7 mg

Scrambled Tofu

Preparation Time: 10 minutes
Cooking Time: 11 minutes
Serve: 4

Ingredients:
- 1 lb extra-firm tofu, drained and pressed
- 1 tsp turmeric
- 1 tbsp lemon juice
- 1 red bell pepper, diced
- 2 garlic cloves, minced
- 1 small onion, diced
- 2 green onions, chopped
- 1/4 cup parsley, chopped
- 1/2 tsp red pepper flakes
- 2 tbsp olive oil

Directions:
1. Heat olive oil in a pan over medium heat.
2. Add onion and sauté for 5 minutes or until softened.
3. Add garlic and sauté for 1 minute.
4. Crumble tofu into the pan and add red pepper flakes, lemon juice, and bell pepper. Stir well and cook for about 5 minutes.
5. Remove pan from heat and fold in green onion, and parsley.
6. Serve and enjoy.

Nutritional Value (Amount per Serving):
- Calories 189
- Fat 13.9 g
- Carbohydrates 8 g
- Sugar 3.2 g
- Protein 12.2 g
- Cholesterol 0 mg

Roasted Mixed Veggies

Preparation Time: 10 minutes
Cooking Time: 25 minutes
Serve: 4

Ingredients:

- 1 cup eggplant, diced
- 1 cup zucchini, sliced
- 1 1/2 tsp garlic, minced
- 1 1/2 tbsp parsley, chopped
- 3 tbsp rice vinegar
- 1 mushroom, sliced
- 8 small asparagus stalks, ends removed
- 2 cups bell pepper, cut into strips
- 1/4 cup olive oil
- 1/2 tsp pepper
- 1 tsp salt

Directions:

1. Preheat the oven 375 F/ 190 C.
2. In a large bowl, whisk together oil, garlic, parsley, pepper, salt, and rice vinegar.
3. Add vegetables in a bowl and toss well.
4. Place vegetables in an aluminum foil pouch and seal Pouch.
5. Bake in preheated oven for 25 minutes.
6. Season with pepper and salt.

Nutritional Value (Amount per Serving):

- Calories 153
- Fat 12.9 g
- Carbohydrates 8.4 g
- Sugar 4.7 g
- Protein 2 g
- Cholesterol 0 mg

Celery Soup

Preparation Time: 10 minutes
Cooking Time: 30 minutes
Serve: 4

Ingredients:

- 6 cups celery
- 1 cup unsweetened coconut milk
- 1 onion, chopped
- 1 tsp dill
- 2 cups of water
- ¼ tsp pepper
- Pinch of salt

Directions:

1. Add all ingredients into the instant pot and stir well.
2. Seal instant pot with a lid and select soup mode.
3. Release pressure using quick release method than open the lid.
4. Puree the soup using an immersion blender until smooth and creamy.
5. Stir well and serve.

Nutritional Value (Amount per Serving):

- Calories 174
- Fat 14.6 g
- Carbohydrates 10.5 g
- Sugar 5.2 g
- Protein 2.8 g
- Cholesterol 0 mg

Garlic Asparagus Soup

Preparation Time: 10 minutes
Cooking Time: 20 minutes
Serve: 4

Ingredients:

- 1/2 cauliflower head, chopped
- 20 asparagus spears, chopped
- 3 garlic cloves, chopped
- 1 tbsp olive oil
- 4 cups vegetable stock
- Pepper
- Salt

Directions:

1. Heat oil in a large saucepan over medium heat.
2. Add garlic and sauté until softened.
3. Add cauliflower, vegetable stock, pepper, and salt. Stir well and bring to boil.
4. Turn heat to low and simmer for 20 minutes.
5. Add chopped asparagus and cook until softened.
6. Puree the soup using an immersion blender until smooth and creamy.
7. Stir and serve.

Nutritional Value (Amount per Serving):

- Calories 74
- Fat 5.6 g
- Carbohydrates 8.9 g
- Sugar 5.1 g
- Protein 3.4 g
- Cholesterol 2 mg

Tomato Soup

Preparation Time: 10 minutes
Cooking Time: 10 minutes
Serve: 4

Ingredients:

- 28 oz can tomato
- 2 tbsp erythritol
- 1/2 tsp garlic powder
- 1/2 tsp onion powder
- 1/4 cup basil pesto
- 1/4 tsp dried basil leaves
- 1 tsp apple cider vinegar
- 2 cups of water
- 1 1/2 tsp kosher salt

Directions:

1. Add tomatoes, garlic powder, onion powder, water, and salt in a saucepan. Bring to boil over medium heat.
2. Turn heat to low and simmer for 2 minutes.
3. Remove saucepan from heat and puree the soup using a blender until smooth.
4. Stir in pesto, dried basil, vinegar, and erythritol.
5. Stir well and serve.

Nutritional Value (Amount per Serving):

- Calories 30
- Fat 0 g
- Carbohydrates 12.1 g
- Sugar 9.6 g
- Protein 1.3 g
- Cholesterol 0 mg

Roasted Broccoli

Preparation Time: 10 minutes
Cooking Time: 20 minutes
Serve: 4

Ingredients:

- 1 1/2 lbs broccoli florets
- 1 tbsp fresh lemon juice
- 3 tbsp almonds, sliced and toasted
- 2 garlic cloves, sliced
- 3 tbsp extra virgin olive oil
- 1/4 tsp pepper
- 1/4 tsp salt

Directions:

1. Preheat the oven to 425 F/ 218 C.
2. Spray a baking tray with cooking spray.
3. Add broccoli, pepper, salt, garlic, and oil in a large bowl and toss well.
4. Spread broccoli on the prepared baking tray and roast in preheated oven for 20 minutes.
5. Add lemon juice and almonds over broccoli and toss well.
6. Serve and enjoy.

Nutritional Value (Amount per Serving):

- Calories 177
- Fat 13.3 g
- Carbohydrates 12.9 g
- Sugar 3.2 g
- Protein 5.8 g
- Cholesterol 0 mg

Chapter 12: Desserts

Chocó Muffins

Preparation Time: 10 minutes
Cooking Time: 20 minutes
Serve: 12

Ingredients:

- 4 eggs
- 1 tsp vanilla
- ¼ cup butter
- 1 tsp baking powder
- ¼ cup heavy cream
- ¼ cup erythritol
- 1 oz unsweetened chocolate chips
- 1 oz unsweetened chocolate, chopped
- ¼ cup unsweetened cocoa powder
- ½ cup almond flour
- Pinch of salt

Directions:

1. Spray a muffin tray with cooking spray and set aside.
2. In a bowl, mix together almond flour, baking powder, sweetener, cocoa powder, and salt.
3. In a separate bowl, beat together butter and heavy cream.
4. Add vanilla and eggs and beat until well combined.
5. Add almond flour mixture to the egg mixture and mix well to combine.
6. Add chopped chocolate and chocolate chips and fold well.
7. Pour batter in a prepared muffin tray and bake at 350 F/ 180 C for 20 minutes.
8. Serve and enjoy.

Nutritional Value (Amount per Serving):

- Calories 123
- Fat 11.3 g
- Carbohydrates 3.7 g
- Sugar 0.4 g
- Protein 3.9 g
- Cholesterol 68 mg

Chia Strawberry Pudding

Preparation Time: 10 minutes
Cooking Time: 10 minutes
Serve: 4

Ingredients:

- 1 tsp unsweetened cocoa powder
- 5 tbsp chia seeds
- 2 tbsp xylitol
- 1 1/2 tsp vanilla
- 1 ½ cups strawberries, chopped
- 1 cup unsweetened coconut milk
- Pinch of salt

Directions:

1. In a saucepan, combine together strawberries, ½ cup water, xylitol, vanilla, and salt and simmer over medium heat for 5-10 minutes.
2. Mash strawberries with a fork.
3. Add coconut milk and stir to combine.
4. Add chia seeds and mix well and let it sit for 5 minutes.
5. Pour pudding mixture in serving glasses.
6. Sprinkle cocoa powder on top of chia pudding.
7. Place in refrigerator for 1 hour.
8. Serve chilled and enjoy.

Nutritional Value (Amount per Serving):

- Calories 211
- Fat 17.4 g
- Carbohydrates 11 g
- Sugar 4.9 g
- Protein 3.8 g
- Cholesterol 0 mg

Cinnamon Protein Bars

Preparation Time: 10 minutes
Cooking Time: 10 minutes
Serve: 8

Ingredients:

- 2 scoops vanilla protein powder
- 1/4 cup coconut oil, melted
- 1 cup almond butter
- 1/4 tsp cinnamon
- 12 drops liquid stevia
- Pinch of salt

Directions:

1. In a bowl, mix together all ingredients until well combined.
2. Transfer bar mixture into a baking dish and press down evenly.
3. Place in refrigerator until firm.
4. Slice and serve.

Nutritional Value (Amount per Serving):

- Calories 99
- Fat 8 g
- Carbohydrates 0.6 g
- Sugar 0.2 g
- Protein 7.2 g
- Cholesterol 0 mg

Chocolate Cake

Preparation Time: 10 minutes
Cooking Time: 30 minutes
Serve: 12

Ingredients:

- 5 large eggs
- 1 1/2 cup erythritol
- 10 oz unsweetened chocolate, melted
- 1/2 cup almond flour
- 10 oz butter, melted
- Pinch of salt

Directions:

1. Preheat the oven to 350 F/ 180 C.
2. Grease spring-form cake pan with butter and set aside.
3. In a large bowl, beat eggs until foamy.
4. Add erythritol and stir well.
5. Add melted butter, chocolate, almond flour, and salt and stir to combine.
6. Pour batter in the prepared cake pan and bake in preheated oven for 30 minutes.
7. Remove cake from oven and allow to cool completely.
8. Slice and serve.

Nutritional Value (Amount per Serving):

- Calories 344
- Fat 35 g
- Carbohydrates 8 g
- Sugar 0.6 g
- Protein 6.9 g
- Cholesterol 128 mg

Raspberry Almond Tart

Preparation Time: 10 minutes
Cooking Time: 23 minutes
Serve: 4

Ingredients:

- 5 egg whites
- 1 tsp vanilla
- 1 1/2 cups raspberries
- 1 lemon zest, grated
- 1 cup almond flour
- 1/2 cup Swerve
- 1/2 cup butter, melted
- 1 tsp baking powder

Directions:

1. Preheat the oven to 375 F/ 190 C.
2. Grease tart tin with cooking spray and set aside.
3. In a large bowl, whisk egg whites until foamy.
4. Add sweetener, baking powder, vanilla, lemon zest, and almond flour and mix until well combined.
5. Add melted butter and stir well.
6. Pour batter in prepared tart tin and top with raspberries.
7. Bake in preheated oven for 20-23 minutes.
8. Serve and enjoy.

Nutritional Value (Amount per Serving):

- Calories 378
- Fat 8 g
- Carbohydrates 14 g
- Sugar 4 g
- Protein 11 g

Pumpkin Pie

Preparation Time: 10 minutes
Cooking Time: 30 minutes
Serve: 4

Ingredients:

- 3 eggs
- 1/2 cup pumpkin puree
- 1/2 tsp cinnamon
- 1/2 tsp vanilla
- 1/4 cup Swerve
- 1/2 cup cream
- 1/2 cup unsweetened almond milk

Directions:

1. Preheat the oven to 350 F/ 180 C.
2. Spray a square baking dish with cooking spray and set aside.
3. In a large bowl, add all ingredients and whisk until smooth.
4. Pour pie mixture into the prepared dish and bake in preheated oven for 30 minutes.
5. Remove from oven and set aside to cool completely.
6. Place into the refrigerator for 1-2 hours.
7. Cut into the pieces and serve.

Nutritional Value (Amount per Serving):

- Calories 84
- Fat 5.5 g
- Carbohydrates 4.4 g
- Sugar 1.9 g
- Protein 4.9 g
- Cholesterol 128 mg

Vanilla Ice Cream

Preparation Time: 10 minutes
Cooking Time: 30 minutes
Serve: 8

Ingredients:

- 1 egg yolk
- 3/4 cup erythritol
- 2 cups heavy whipping cream
- 1 tsp vanilla
- 3 tsp cinnamon
- Pinch of salt

Directions:

1. Add all ingredients to the mixing bowl and blend until well combined.
2. Pour ice cream mixture into the ice cream maker and churn ice cream according to the machine instructions.
3. Serve and enjoy.

Nutritional Value (Amount per Serving):

- Calories 114
- Fat 11.7 g
- Carbohydrates 1.7 g
- Sugar 0.1 g
- Protein 1 g
- Cholesterol 67 mg

Fresh Berry Yogurt

Preparation Time: 10 minutes
Cooking Time: 10 minutes
Serve: 6

Ingredients:

- 1 tsp vanilla
- 1 cup coconut cream
- 1 cup mixed berries
- 2 tbsp erythritol
- 1/2 lemon juice

Directions:

1. In a bowl, mix together coconut cream, sweetener, lemon juice, and vanilla and place in the refrigerator for 30 minutes.
2. Add berries and frozen coconut cream mixture into the blender and blend until smooth.
3. Transfer blended mixture in container and place in the refrigerator for 1-2 hours.
4. Serve and enjoy.

Nutritional Value (Amount per Serving):

- Calories 100
- Fat 9 g
- Carbohydrates 5 g
- Sugar 3.2 g
- Protein 1 g
- Cholesterol 0 mg

Cheese Berry Fat Bomb

Preparation Time: 5 minutes
Cooking Time: 5 minutes
Serve: 12

Ingredients:

- 1 cup fresh berries, wash
- 1/2 cup coconut oil
- 1 1/2 cup cream cheese, softened
- 1 tbsp vanilla
- 2 tbsp swerve

Directions:

1. Add all ingredients to the blender and blend until smooth and combined.
2. Spoon mixture into small candy molds and refrigerate until set.
3. Serve and enjoy.

Nutritional Value (Amount per Serving):

- Calories 175
- Fat 17 g
- Carbohydrates 2 g
- Sugar 1 g
- Protein 2.1 g
- Cholesterol 29 mg

Chocó Cookies

Preparation Time: 10 minutes
Cooking Time: 10 minutes
Serve: 14

Ingredients:

- 1 egg
- 1/2 cup erythritol
- 1/4 cup unsweetened cocoa powder
- 1 cup almond butter
- 3 tbsp unsweetened almond milk
- 1/4 cup unsweetened chocolate chips

Directions:

1. Preheat the oven to 350 F/ 180 C.
2. Line baking tray with parchment paper and set aside.
3. In a bowl, mix together almond butter, egg, sweetener, almond milk, and cocoa powder until well combined.
4. Stir in Chocó chips.
5. Make cookies from mixture and place on a prepared baking tray.
6. Bake for 10 minutes.
7. Allow to cool completely then serve.

Nutritional Value (Amount per Serving):

- Calories 44
- Fat 3.5 g
- Carbohydrates 2.2 g
- Sugar 0.1 g
- Protein 1.5 g
- Cholesterol 12 mg

Conclusion

This book is perfect for keto diet beginners, you will get everything in this book not only preparing recipes but also, we have seen how the ketogenic diet is different from other diet and what are the health benefits of the diet in detail with enjoying different types of delicious and healthy keto recipes.

In this book, you will get 79 delicious and healthy keto recipes that are easy to prepare.

Made in the USA
Middletown, DE
06 May 2020

93830134R00066